walking with purpose

Dear Friend,

Do you feel there's more demanded of you than you can possibly get done each day? Is there a lot on your plate, and are some things falling off? Do you want to slow down and give a little time to your heart and spiritual life? We're here to help. We get it. We've put together this booklet to give you a taste of our life-changing course, *Opening Your Heart*. We've chosen some of our favorite lessons, and offer them in this format so you can get a taste of our transformative material.

So much of your time is spent giving to others. Receive this little booklet as a gift to yourself. Open it up. Don't overwhelm yourself by thinking that you've got to make a huge commitment. Just set a small goal and see what you can do in ten days. Give God a little bit of time each day as you move through these lessons. I promise you, He will not be outdone in generosity. He never is.

How I wish I could place this booklet directly into your hands and tell you how much you are loved and treasured by God. You might already know that, or you might doubt it with every fiber of your being. Regardless of where you are at, God will meet you right where you are. He doesn't ask you to clean up first or hustle to prove your worth. He just says *come*.

With prayers for you as you open your heart to the One who loves you best ~

Lisa Brenninkmeyer
Founder and Chief Purpose Officer of Walking with Purpose

Opening Your Heart
Sample Booklet

www.walkingwithpurpose.com

Authored by Lisa Brenninkmeyer

IMPRIMATUR + William E. Lori, S.T.D., Archbishop of Baltimore

The recommended Bible translations for use in Walking with Purpose studies are: The Revised Standard Version, Catholic Edition; The New American Bible, which is the translation used in the United States for the readings at Mass; and The Jerusalem Bible.

Any internet addresses (websites, blogs, etc.) in this book are offered as a resource, and may change in the future. Please refer to www.walkingwithpurpose.com as the central location for corresponding materials and references.

22 23 24 25/12 11 10 9 8 7 6

ISBN: 978-1-943173-07-5
Opening Your Heart Sample Booklet

Printed in the United States of America

Opening Your Heart Sample Booklet

TABLE OF CONTENTS

INTRODUCTION

SAMPLE LESSONS

APPENDICES

These sample lessons have been taken from our full course *Opening Your Heart: The Starting Point*.
For a full listing of other topics covered in the 22-lesson study guide, please see page number 3.

The guided tour of God's love begins here.

Opening Your Heart: The Starting Point begins a woman's exploration of her Catholic faith and enhances her relationship with Jesus Christ. This Bible study is designed to inspire thoughtful consideration of the fundamental questions of living a life in the Lord. More than anything, it's a weekly practice of opening your heart to the only One who can heal and transform lives.

Explore these topics and more:

- What is the role of the Holy Spirit in my life?
- What does the Eucharist have to do with my friendship with Christ?
- What are the limits of Christ's forgiveness?
- Why and how should I pray?
- What is the purpose of suffering?
- What challenges will I face in my efforts to follow Jesus more closely?
- How can fear be overcome?

A companion video series complements this journey with practical insights and spiritual support.

Opening Your Heart is a foundational 22-lesson Bible study that serves any woman who seeks to grow closer to God. It's an ideal starting point for women who are new to Walking with Purpose and those with prior practice in Bible study, too.

Opening Your Heart, Full Course

TOPICS

Who Is Jesus Christ?

Why Is Jesus Christ Interested in My Friendship?

Why and How Should I Pray?

Who Is the Holy Spirit?

Why Should I Read the Bible?

What Is Grace and What Difference Does It Make?

What Are the Limits of Christ's Forgiveness?

What Does the Sacrament of Penance Have to Do with My Friendship with Christ?

What Does the Eucharist Have to Do with My Friendship with Christ?

How Can I Conquer My Fears?

What Is the Role of Suffering in My Life?

What Does Mary Have to Do with My Relationship with Christ?

Can God Really Change Me or Is That Just Wishful Thinking?

What Challenges Will I Face in My Efforts to Follow Jesus More Closely?

What Is the Relevance of the Church in My Life?

How Do I Read the Bible in a Meaningful Way?

Welcome to Walking with Purpose

You have many choices when it comes to how you spend your time – thank you for choosing to try Walking with Purpose. Studying God's Word with an open and receptive heart will bring spiritual growth and enrichment to all aspects of your life, making every moment that you've invested well worth it.

Each one of us comes to this material from our own unique vantage point. You are welcome as you are. No experience is necessary. Some of you will find that the questions in this sample booklet cause you to think about concepts that are new to you. Others might find much is a review. God meets each one of us where we are, and He is always faithful, taking us to a deeper, better place spiritually, regardless of where we begin.

The Structure of *Opening Your Heart Sample Booklet*

Opening Your Heart Sample Booklet is a Bible study that includes **two** of our favorite lessons from our 22-lesson course, *Opening Your Heart: The Starting Point.* The lessons integrate Scripture with the teachings of the Roman Catholic Church to point us to principles that help us manage life's pace and pressure while living with calm and steadiness.

This booklet is designed to give you a taste of our life-changing course, *Opening Your Heart,* through interactive personal study. We hope you enjoy it!

Sample Booklet Format and Reference Materials

Opening Your Heart Sample Booklet is divided into two sections:

The first section comprises two lessons. The lessons are divided into five "days" to help you form a habit of reading and reflecting on God's Word regularly. If you are a woman who has only bits and pieces of time throughout your day to accomplish tasks, you will find this breakdown of lessons especially helpful. Each day focuses on Scripture readings and related teaching passages, and ends with a Quiet Your Heart reflection. In addition, Day Five includes a Saint's Story; a lesson conclusion; a resolution section, in which you set a goal for yourself based on a theme of the lesson; and short clips from the *Catechism of the Catholic Church (CCC)*, which are referenced throughout the lesson to complement the Scripture study.

The second section, the appendices, includes an article about Saint Thérèse of Lisieux, the patron saint of Walking with Purpose (Appendix 1). Appendix 2 is the article "Conversion of Heart". Appendix 3 is the answer key. You will benefit so much more from the study lessons if you work through the questions on your own, searching your heart, as this is your very personal journey of faith. The answer key is meant to provide personal guidance or insight when needed.

Walking with Purpose™ Website

Please visit our website at www.walkingwithpurpose.com to find additional free content, supplemental materials that complement our Bible studies, as well as a link to our online store for additional Bible studies, DVDs, books, and more!

WWP *Scripture Printables* of our exclusively designed verse cards that compliment all Bible studies. They are available in various sizes and formats, perfect for lock screens or emailing to a friend.

WWP *Playlists* of Founder Lisa Brenninkmeyer's favorite music accompany each Bible study.

WWP *Videos* of all Connect Coffee talks.

WWP *Blog* for a weekly dose of inspiration and encouragement from our bloggers. Subscribe for updates.

WWP *Leadership Development Program*

Do you long to see more women touched by the love of Christ, but you aren't sure how you can help? We are here to help you learn the art of creating community. It's easier than you think! God doesn't call the equipped; He equips the called. If you love God and love women, then you have what it takes to make a difference in the lives of people around you. Through our training, you'll be empowered to step out of your comfort zone and experience the rush of serving God with passion and purpose. You are not alone, and you can become a great leader. We offer the encouragement and the tools you need to reach out to a world that desperately needs to experience the love of God.

Join Us on Social Media

facebook.com/walkingwithpurpose

twitter.com/walkingwpurpose

instagram.com/walkingwithpurpose_official

youtube.com/walkingwithpurpose_official

pinterest.com/walkingwpurpose

Lessons

Walking with Purpose is a community of women growing in faith – together! This is where women are gathering. Join us!

www.walkingwithpurpose.com

Lesson 1

WHAT IS GRACE AND WHAT DIFFERENCE DOES IT MAKE?

Introduction

We use the word *grace* in many different ways. The prayer before dinner is called grace, a woman of elegance and poise has grace, a dignified man with polite manners has grace, and one can grace a party with his or her presence.

We can give grace to our children. A number of years ago, my husband and I received a phone call from our son's school saying that he had been caught cheating on a test and had been suspended as a result. My husband picked our son up at school and brought him to his office. One of the consequences he gave our son was spending the day writing the words "I will never cheat again" five hundred times. He wrote for hours, wisely not complaining. By five o'clock in the evening, it was clear that there weren't enough hours left in the day to finish the writing. My husband decided to give grace, not by saying that the writing didn't need to be done, but by sitting down and writing alongside our son. Together, they finished the five hundred sentences, and drove home.

So what does grace mean in the spiritual sense? The Catechism defines it as follows:

"Grace is favor, the free and undeserved help that God gives to respond to His call to become children of God, adoptive sons [and daughters], partakers of the divine nature and of eternal life." (CCC 1996)

The *Encarta World English Dictionary* defines grace as the infinite love, mercy, favor, and goodwill shown to humankind by God.

The grace my husband gave our son, which is the grace God gives to His children, is free and undeserved help. Both show love and mercy. But God's grace given to us far surpasses anything that we can show to one another. He doesn't just come alongside us, *sharing* the punishment that our sins deserve. He takes on Himself the *entire* punishment due us. After paying that price, He offers us the gift of being His children and spending eternity with Him. The Giver of All Good Things doesn't stop there. He cares about each one of us so personally that He offers us grace each and every day for all of our varied circumstances.

But before we dive in, I've got to warn you . . .

You have to gear up for this lesson, ladies. It plunges you into some theology that at first glance might make you want to yawn or cross your eyes. Stick with it. Don't be put off by vocab that may be new to you. Because hidden within these meaty passages is the stuff that we are longing for.

Day One
THE FIRST WORK OF GRACE

1. According to CCC 1989, what is the first work of the grace of the Holy Spirit? What moves man to turn toward God and away from sin?

Grace's first work is to draw your heart toward God. That first time you felt hungry to learn more about spiritual things? That was grace at work. That sense you get in your gut that what you are doing isn't really in your best interest, that God wants something different and better for you? That is grace at work.

God is always after your heart. But He never blasts through and forces Himself on you. He's gentle, and recognizes that conversion is a gradual process. He'll let you run after the things that you think will satisfy, and He'll wait. When you figure out that you want more, but view Him as an "add-on," as one thing among many that you hope will fill you up, He'll wait patiently. When you come to the point where you recognize He is the only One who can satisfy you, grace will rush in and you'll receive "grace upon grace." (John 1:16)

2. Grace does something else as well—it results in justification. List the descriptions of *justification* found in CCC 1989 and 1990.

In other words . . .

Justification throws our sins as far away from us as the east is from the west. (Psalm 103:12)

Justification renews the inner parts of us—the parts that are wounded and hurting and hidden. (2 Corinthians 4:16)

Justification makes us clean—as white as freshly fallen snow. (Isaiah 1:18)

Justification reconciles us with God. (2 Corinthians 5:19)

Justification gives us what we need to break free from the bondage of habits that destroy us. (Galatians 5:1)

Justification heals us. (1 Peter 2:24)

And it's grace at work in our souls that results in justification. Without grace, we wouldn't be able to experience any of these things.

3. According to Titus 3:4–7, how are we saved? Why did God pour out the Holy Spirit on us?

4. Grace's first work is drawing us to a point of conversion. The effect of conversion is justification. What do we need to do to experience all the benefits of justification? Think about your answer to question 3, and see CCC 1991.

Quiet your heart and enjoy His presence. . . . He wants to give you "grace upon grace."

I don't know about you, but when I read about all the grace that God wants to pour over me through justification, I wonder why the heck I run after so much emptiness. Why do I think that distracting myself, or numbing myself, or losing five pounds is really going to fix the things that aren't working in my life? What I really want is healing. Freedom. A fresh start. And that's what God is offering me—using the word grace *to describe it all. Let's reach out and grasp it with both hands.*

Dear Lord,

I really want all the grace that you have for me. But I've got some things in my hands that I'm going to have to put down if I'm going to be able to receive it from you. Help me to lay down my self-reliance. Help me to lay down my desire to keep everyone happy—my habit of people pleasing. Help me to lay down my determination to always be comfortable. Sometimes I have to get uncomfortable for a while in order to experience all you have for me. Help me to remember Saint Augustine's words: "God gives where he finds empty hands."

Day Two
THE EXTRAVAGANCE OF GRACE

1. Is the grace of salvation something that we earn? See Romans 11:6 and Ephesians 2:8–9.

2. If we don't merit salvation (justification) because of our good works, does that mean grace is cheap? Does it come at no cost? See CCC 1992.

The grace of our salvation has come to us at an enormous cost: Christ's life. Jesus stepped in and took the punishment that was due each one of us. He didn't do this because our good works make us worth it. He deems us "worth it" simply because He loves us. He asks us to have confidence (faith) in *His* payment for our sins, instead of our own attempts to pay for them. "A man is justified by faith apart from works of the law." (Romans 3:28)

3. What is the source of our merits (our abilities, our achievements, our worth) before God? What role does grace play in this? See CCC 2011. Note: In this context, the word *charity* means "love."

When you think about it, there really is nothing for us to boast about. Even the good things that we do (our "merits") find their source in the love of Christ that He has put in our hearts. We stand before God because of what Christ has done on our behalf, not because of what we have done for ourselves. God pours out extravagant grace, and we are the fortunate recipients.

4. We can't deny that the grace God gives us is free and undeserved. So why do you think we find it so hard to offer grace to others?

Quiet your heart and enjoy His presence. . . . The price has been paid. Rest in His grace.

We've grown up hearing that there's "no such thing as a free lunch." And so we set out to earn our place in the world. We eat our vegetables to earn dessert. We get good grades to earn good college placement. We get the internship to earn the job. We get the gym membership to earn the better body, which we hope will earn us the guy of our dreams. Everything worth having comes at a cost, and we are exhausted trying to get and keep it all.

God speaks into our weariness. He asks us to let go of the "try hard" life. He offers us His grace, and asks us to offer it to others in turn. Spend some time talking to God about what area of your life feels exhausting. Ask Him to help you let go of expectations—those others have for you and those you have for others. Ask Him to replace the expectations with gratitude for the grace He extravagantly pours over you.

Day Three
THE RISK OF GRACE

"But where sin increased, grace abounded all the more." (Romans 5:20)

When we read of the extravagance of grace, we recognize there's a risk. Won't people take advantage of this? Won't they be tempted to say, "Yes, I know this is wrong. But I'm going to do it anyway and ask for forgiveness later"? As Herod said in W. H. Auden's poem *For the Time Being*, "Every crook will argue: 'I like committing crimes. God likes forgiving them. Really, the world is admirably arranged.'"[1]

Which brings us to the question, "Why be good?" This is exactly the question Saint Paul addresses in the New Testament book of Romans.

1. According to Romans 6:14, why is sin not to have power over us?

2. Read Romans 3:19–20. According to verse 19, why was the law given? What does verse 20 say we become conscious of through the law?

Let's unpack the phrase "under the law." This describes the way God's people lived before Christ's death and Resurrection. God had given them laws to live by. The purpose of these laws was to help them make choices that would keep them healthy, both spiritually and physically. But time and time again, God's people failed to follow the laws. They were unable to live up to those standards.

This is what Saint Paul was talking about in Romans 3:19 when he said that the law was given so that we'd all be silenced. We're silenced because we are aware of how much we fall short of God's standard of holiness. The alternative to being silenced is to justify ourselves by saying, "Look at how good I am! Can you see all the things I've done? I've earned your love, God!" The law acts as a mirror, and when we hold it up to ourselves, our voices fall silent as we see that we haven't been able to obey all that God has asked of us. Living under the law is hard, because we simply don't have what it takes to do it.

---

[1] W. H. Auden, *For the Time Being: A Christmas Oratorio* (Princeton, NJ: Princeton University Press, 2013), 57.

3. Romans 6:14 tells us that as Christians, we don't live under the law. We live under grace. Living under grace is living under a *new* law. According to CCC 1966, what is the new law?

This brings us back to the question, "Why be good?" The answer? *Because we can be.* Because everything is different now that the Holy Spirit dwells in us. What we cannot do for ourselves, the Holy Spirit will do *in us and for us*, if we ask Him. Please don't just speed past these words. Let the truth they contain sink in.

In the words of Father Jacques Philippe, "According to grace, we receive salvation and the love of God freely through Christ, quite apart from our merits, and freely respond to that love by the good works the Holy Spirit enables us to accomplish."[2] The law is not the foundation of our relationship with God; love is. It is love that motivates us to ask the Holy Spirit to help us live in the way that God desires.

4. What is an area of your life where you have been aware of falling short of what God desires to see in you? Have you been trying to "create your own goodness" instead of relying on the Holy Spirit to do the work in and through you? What do you think indicates a person is relying on him- or herself instead of on God to grow in holiness?

Quiet your heart and enjoy His presence. . . . Let Him infuse your heart with the grace to obey.

"What then? Are we to sin because we are not under the law but under grace? By no means!" (Romans 6:15)

Some people look at grace as the ticket that allows them to live however they want and just ask for forgiveness later. This kind of behavior can result when we look at God's instructions to us as ways He's trying to take away all our fun. But nothing could be further from the truth. Our heavenly Father wants us to be happy and satisfied. The commandments He gives us are there for our protection and to lead us to a place of health and wholeness. Why would we want to sin? It only leads to unhappiness.

---

[2] Jacques Philippe, *Interior Freedom* (New York: Scepter Publishers, 2002), 114.

Take some time to prayerfully think about an area in your life where you find it hard to do things "God's way." Ponder the fact that all He wants is what is best for you. Ask Him to help you to trust that obedience is what will truly make you happy.

Day Four
THE SUFFICIENCY OF GRACE

1. Saint Paul wrote a letter to the church in Corinth, and in it, he talked about a thorn in his flesh that he begged God to get rid of. How did God answer his request? See 2 Corinthians 12:9.

The phrase "is made perfect" means "is given most fully and manifests itself fully."[3] Isn't that amazing? When we are at our weakest, God's power is most fully given and manifests itself most fully. That's a truth to cling to when we're at the end of our resources.

2. When we are in need of grace, we can immediately turn to God in prayer, and He will meet us in our place of weakness. Where else can we go to receive grace? See CCC 1966.

Even when we are struggling with a thorn in our side, God still asks us to love. He doesn't ask us to scrape the bottom of the barrel of our own resources and just do the best we can. He asks us to drink from His endless supply of grace, poured out on us through the sacraments.

Sometimes all we can do is lift up weary, empty hands and ask for the filling of His grace. I can remember a particularly difficult time of my life, when I could barely find the strength to pray. I knew I needed to persevere in loving my family, but the most

---

[3] 2 Corinthians 12:9 footnote, in New American Bible, Revised Edition (Washington, DC: Confraternity of Christian Doctrine, 2010), 274.

basic things seemed so very hard. My prayer became little more than the outstretching of my empty hands. My words were few, but the physical action meant a lot. It was my way of telling the Lord that I had nothing to offer, and I needed Him to fill me with His grace. I went to daily Mass, and found that simply putting my body in a place where I could receive grace had an enormous impact on my spirit. I believe the Eucharist gave me the strength that I lacked. Bit by bit, I was restored.

3. What "thorn" is in your side right now? I'd guess that you, like Saint Paul, would like God to just take that thorn away. Perhaps He will. Sometimes He does. But other times, He allows the thorn to stay, in order to accomplish His purposes in us. Why was Saint Paul able to deal with his thorn? See 2 Corinthians 12:10.

Quiet your heart and enjoy His presence. . . . "Be strong in the grace that is in Christ Jesus." (2 Timothy 2:1)

"They who wait for the LORD shall renew their strength, they shall mount up with wings like eagles, they shall run and not be weary, they shall walk and not faint." (Isaiah 40:31)

Dear Lord,

This is where our hope lies. It lies in you. The renewal and strength that we long for doesn't come from the spa or from perfect circumstances. It shows up when we have nothing to offer, and fills up our empty hands. Thank you for the grace that strengthens and sustains us. Thank you for making it so that at any time and in any place, we can "with confidence draw near to the throne of grace, that we may receive mercy and find grace to help in time of need." (Hebrews 4:16)

Day Five
SAINT'S STORY

Saint Josephine Bakhita

Sudan is a land well acquainted with suffering, having been bathed in the blood of genocide and ravaged by slave traders for many years. Josephine Bakhita was born in Olgossa, in the Darfur region of southern Sudan, in 1869. When she was eleven, she was kidnapped and sold into slavery. The trauma of being ripped from her family and sold and resold repeatedly was such that she forgot her own name; in its place, she was given the name Bakhita—ironically, meaning "fortunate."

Josephine Bakhita's life seems anything but fortunate. One of her masters' sons beat her so severely, she could not move from her straw bed for a month. Another master, an Ottoman Army officer, marked her as his property by scarring her body and tattooing her with more than sixty patterns on her breasts, belly, and arms. She was also forcibly converted to Islam.

Different masters took her all over Africa, and eventually to Venice, Italy. God was working through the circumstances of Josephine Bakhita's life, and it was here, through the Canossian Sisters in Venice, that she first heard the words of Jesus: "Come to me, all who labor and are heavy laden, and I will give you rest. Take my yoke upon you, and learn from me; for I am gentle and lowly of heart, and you will find rest for your souls. For my yoke is easy, and my burden is light." (Matthew 11:28–30) The heart recognizes the truth in such words of gentleness. By 1890, she was baptized and had taken the Italian Christian name Giuseppina Margarita (Josephine Margaret in English).

A few years later, when her owner wanted to return to Africa, Josephine Bakhita refused to go. The Canossian Sisters and the Patriarch of Venice interceded on her behalf, and guaranteed her the freedom of choice contained in Italian law. Legally in Italy, she was a free woman, the mistress of her own destiny. But in reality, she had become a free woman from the moment of her baptism in 1890. Even in her final years as a slave, she knew that the gift of baptismal grace had already set her free on the inside: "If the Son makes you free, you will be free indeed." (John 8:36) With Christ living inside her by grace, she knew that nothing except sin could ever enslave her again.

With her newfound legal freedom, Josephine Bakhita became a Canossian Sister. In 1893, she entered the convent, and in 1896, she made her profession. A young student once asked her, "What would you do, if you were to meet your captors?"

Showing true grace and understanding, she answered, "If I were to meet those who kidnapped me, and even those who tortured me, I would kneel and kiss their hands. For, if these things had not happened, I would not have been a Christian and a religious today." With this spirit of gratitude and humility, she worked hard doing menial tasks in the convent, often saying, "Be good, love the Lord, and pray for those who do not know Him. What a great grace it is to know God!"

Josephine Bakhita would pray that you, too, would know this great grace and hold it in high esteem. Grace is the gentle Lordship of Jesus Christ. It is His life flowing through our veins, His heart beating inside ours. Grace is what sets us free from slavery and gives us our true dignity. It is what makes us daughters of the King. You are a daughter of the King, and your heart will always be free if you live in His grace.

As you read and reflect on Saint Josephine Bakhita's story, consider how she was able to experience inner freedom despite the outward conditions of slavery that marked the early years of her life. Does this change your appreciation of Christ's grace?

Conclusion

Have you ever felt a heaviness of heart, a sense of despair, or a deep-seated fear that your life will never get better? I remember a period of my life when discouragement and depression nearly blotted out my ability to feel God's grace.

My husband and I had been living in Mexico for a number of years. Something was making me physically ill; whether it was a parasite or emotional unrest, I never knew the cause. I spent a week each month in my bed, unable to keep any food in my system. I longed to go home, as I missed the United States terribly. When we were robbed by someone very close to us, the betrayal felt overwhelming. I felt unsafe, unsettled, and uncared for. Everything made me cry, and each morning when I woke, I longed to pull the covers over my head and escape back into sleep.

All was made more complicated by the fact that I had four children who needed a mother who was strong and loving, and who created a safe environment for them. I realized that my emotional state was not only taking me closer and closer to a dark pit, but it was harming my children.

On one of my lowest days, I read this verse in Psalm 51:14, NAB: "Restore unto me the joy of my salvation." I realized that I had been given such amazing grace when God gave me salvation, but that I wanted *more*. Where was my gratitude? Why could I not appreciate all that He had given me in dying on the cross for my sins? How could I expect more from the person who gave His life for me? I knew God wanted me to experience joy because He had saved me. But how could I drum up feelings I didn't have? It seemed impossible. I was empty.

I sensed Jesus listening to the cries of my heart and saying, "With man this is impossible, but with God all things are possible." (Matthew 19:26) His grace was being offered to me: grace to help me to be grateful for what I had; grace to get up and be the kind of mother my children needed even though I wanted to do nothing but cry and sleep; grace to encourage my husband and smile at him even though I thought it was his fault that we had to live in a place I hated; and grace to quit complaining about all I didn't like because it was only making me feel worse.

I knelt before God that day and said, "God, I know I should feel joy because of my salvation, but I don't. I just feel unhappy. Please, will you do the work of restoring that joy to me? I can't do it myself. I do promise this: I will quit complaining about all that I don't like in Mexico. I'll quit complaining to other people, but also to you. I'll stop asking you to bring me back home. But I only promise because I know that you don't forget anything. You know the desires of my heart. Even if I'm not reminding you, you know. I will try to trust that if you don't change my circumstances, you know what is best for me. But help me. I am so weak."

The progress was slow, but after about three months, I realized I was much better. I didn't cry so much; I could delight in little things; the peace of my heart was returning. And just when I thought, "It's OK. I can live here. I'm all right," my husband quit his job and told me he was taking me home.

I am so grateful that God led me through the valley of despair before giving me what I desired. What I learned along the way was such a gift. God's grace is enough.

"I know how to be abased, and I know how to abound; in any and all circumstances I have learned the secret of facing plenty and hunger, abundance and want. I can do all things in him who strengthens me." (Philippians 4:12–13)

My Resolution

In what specific way will I apply what I have learned in this lesson?

Examples:

1. I want to experience all the grace that God has for me. I'll grab hold of the opportunity for more of His grace by going to Mass one additional time this week.

2. If I am feeling discouraged about an area in my life where I repeatedly make the same mistakes, I'll increase my prayer about that struggle. Instead of trying harder, I will pray more.

3. I will write 2 Corinthians 12:9 on an index card and carry it with me to remind myself that in my weakness, God is strong.

My Resolution:

Catechism Clips

CCC 1966 The New Law is *the grace of the Holy Spirit* given to the faithful through faith in Christ. It works through charity; it uses the Sermon on the Mount to teach us what must be done and makes use of the sacraments to give us the grace to do it.

CCC 1989 The first work of the grace of the Holy Spirit is *conversion*, effecting justification in accordance with Jesus' proclamation at the beginning of the Gospel: "Repent, for the kingdom of heaven is at hand." Moved by grace, man turns toward God and away from sin, thus accepting forgiveness and righteousness from on high. "Justification is not only the remission of sins, but also the sanctification [growth in holiness] and renewal of the interior man."

CCC 1990 Justification *detaches man from sin* which contradicts the love of God, and purifies his heart of sin. Justification follows upon God's merciful initiative of offering forgiveness. It reconciles man with God. It frees from the enslavement to sin, and it heals.

CCC 1991 Justification is at the same time *the acceptance of God's righteousness* through faith in Jesus Christ. Righteousness (or "justice") here means the rectitude of divine love. With justification, faith, hope, and charity are poured into our hearts, and obedience to the divine will is granted us.

CCC 1992 Justification has been merited for us by the Passion of Christ who offered himself on the cross as a living victim, holy and pleasing to God, and whose blood has become the instrument of atonement for the sins of all men. Justification is conferred in Baptism, the sacrament of faith. It conforms us to the righteousness of God, who makes us inwardly just by the power of his mercy. Its purpose is the glory of God and of Christ, and the gift of eternal life:

> But now the righteousness of God has been manifested apart from law, although the law and the prophets bear witness to it, the righteousness of God through faith in Jesus Christ for all who believe. For there is no distinction: since all have sinned and fall short of the glory of God, they are justified by his grace as a gift, through the redemption which is in Christ Jesus, whom God put forward as an expiation by his blood, to be received by faith. This was to show God's righteousness, because in his divine forbearance he had passed over former sins; it was to prove at the present time that he himself is righteous and that he justifies him who has faith in Jesus.

CCC 2011 *The charity of Christ is the source in us of all our merits* before God. Grace, by uniting us to Christ in active love, ensures the supernatural quality of our acts and consequently their merit before God and before men. The saints have always had a lively awareness that their merits were pure grace.

> After earth's exile, I hope to go and enjoy you in the fatherland, but I do not want to lay up merits for heaven. I want to work for your *love alone* . . . In the evening of this life, I shall appear before you with empty hands, for I do not ask you to count my works. All our justice is blemished in your eyes. I wish, then, to be clothed in your own *justice* and to receive from your *love* the eternal possession of *yourself*. —Saint Thérèse of Lisieux

Quit Hustling.
Find Peace.

 Are you ready to trade proving and pleasing for belonging and breathing deeply?

 Are you longing to exhale?

 Are you tired of pressure and longing for joy?

Scan here for a free audio talk on 4 ways to quit hustling and find peace!

This free, exclusive content will put you on the road to your happiest year yet!

NOTES

No program near you? No problem...it's easy to start your own group in your parish or at home and we will walk with you every step of the way. Find out more:

www.walkingwithpurpose.com

Lesson 2

HOW CAN I CONQUER MY FEARS?

Introduction

The storms of the rainy season in Guadalajara, Mexico, were powerful and breathtakingly intense. The kids loved it when we'd take our Suburban out in the midst of a storm. They'd scream with excitement as the water broke over the hood of the car and splashed on their windows, climbing up the sides of the car. Smaller cars would start to float around the roads, out of control. The sensible thing would have been to stay home, but we loved the thrill of being out in the middle of it all, and we had (somewhat groundless) confidence in our Suburban's ability to stay steady no matter what. Our kids liked the rain and the sense of adventure that the storms would bring.

At least that was the case until one particularly crazy storm. We were all at home, enjoying the afternoon, when the rains began. Five-year-old Amy was playing in her bedroom and I was reading in the living room. Bedrooms were on one side of the house, the kitchen on the other, and the two-story, open living room was in the middle with skylights covering most of the ceiling. The rain started calmly enough, but all of a sudden, noises began to explode as hail pelted the skylights. There was a crack, and as I looked up to see the skylights shattering and raining down shards of glass everywhere, Amy appeared at the doorway of her bedroom. Terrified, she began to run through the flying glass to get to me.

And I froze.

I froze. What kind of a mother *freezes* at a time like that? The same mother who knows the Heimlich maneuver yet froze when her three-year-old was choking on a marble. Thank heavens someone with a cool head was nearby to help. I don't know why on earth that has been my reaction not once, but twice, and thank the Lord our brave babysitter was in the kitchen and ran through the glass to rescue Amy. But fear can do that. It can be utterly paralyzing at the absolute worst times imaginable.

Not surprisingly, Amy wasn't so fond of rain after that. And like clockwork, we could count on a daily storm during the rainy season. My response was to comfort her and hold her, to play music loudly during the storms to drown out the sound of the rain. Her daddy's approach was a little different. When the storm would start, he would scoop her up and take her outside. He'd ask her to look at his face, and then he'd smile and talk about how much he loved the rain. He'd stomp in the puddles and make it all a game. Little by little, as she'd watch his lack of fear and total comfort in the storm, she got to the point where she would stomp in the puddles herself. Fear didn't get the last word.

Jesus desires that peace rule in each of our hearts. Yet many people live paralyzed by fear. Panic attacks are on the rise; in any given year, about one-third of American adults have at least one. Sometimes one can see the effects of fear in people in the form of phobias or fearful behavior. But more often, we hide our fears in our hearts. Sometimes even our best friends don't know our secret fears, but they are there, robbing us of the joy that Jesus wants each of us to experience every day. During this lesson, we'll explore ways we can conquer our fears, allowing them to come under the control of God's loving hand.

Day One
AFRAID OF THE STORM

The emotion of fear is a gift insofar as it alerts us to danger. Our senses become heightened, and we look for a way out. Fear lets us know the storm is coming or has hit, but it's not enough to get us *through* the storm. We need something more than that.

Read Matthew 14:22–33.

1. What shift in focus caused Peter to start sinking in the waves? How was he saved from drowning?

2. What kind of a spirit has God given us? See 2 Timothy 1:7.

A spirit of fear will alert us to danger and sharpen our senses, but it will never provide us with what we need to navigate the storms of life. To make it through those circumstances, we need supernatural power, God's unconditional love, and the self-control that helps us choose to dwell on certain things and not others. The good news is, this is exactly what the indwelling Holy Spirit provides. If we replace our spirit of fear with the Spirit of power, love, and self-control, we can conquer our fears.

3. In what ways have you seen God's power in your life? When have you experienced His unconditional love? Has He ever strengthened you by helping you to have self-control in an area of weakness? Share your experiences here and let God's track record of faithfulness increase your confidence in Him. Whatever you face, His presence within you will make all the difference.

Quiet your heart and enjoy His presence. . . . Allow God to dispel your fear.

Fear is unavoidable, but what we choose to do with it is up to us. In the very moment that we feel afraid, we can remind ourselves, "God did not give us a spirit of timidity but a spirit of power and love and self-control." (2 Timothy 1:7) That is what is inside us.

When panic hits, grab hold of Jesus' hand. Lock your eyes on the truth that you are not alone, that He is present, and that His presence makes all the difference. Ask Him to dispel your fear.

"He who dwells in the shelter of the Most High, who abides in the shadow of the Almighty, will say to the Lord, 'My refuge and my fortress; my God, in whom I trust.'" (Psalm 91:1–2)

"I learned that courage was not the absence of fear but the triumph over it. The brave man is not he that doesn't feel afraid, but he who conquers that fear." —Nelson Mandela

Day Two
AFRAID OF WALKING ALONE AT NIGHT

A survey conducted by Chapman University, in California, discovered that one of Americans' greatest fears is walking alone at night.[4] When people answered the survey, they were probably thinking of the dark alley, the dimly lit parking lot—that sort of thing. I understand this fear. Once the sun goes down, I imagine someone is hiding under my car in the mall parking lot, just waiting to slash my ankles. I start to regret that my hair is always in a ponytail because that's easy for some ne'er-do-well to grab. I walk with my finger over the alarm button on my key fob because you just never know. So I get being freaked out at night.

Night can mean all that—or it can be a metaphor for a general darkness in our circumstances or a darkness in our souls. And we are very afraid of walking through those times alone. That's when walking with your hair down and the key fob in hand just doesn't offer much comfort. So what does Scripture have to say to that fear? Let's dive in. There are lots of verses to look up today, friends. But hang with me. You might end up discovering a couple that you'll carry with you from now on.

1. Did Jesus promise that if we follow Him, He'll remove all challenges from our lives? See John 16:33.

2. What did Saint Teresa of Ávila learn from her experience of trusting God in every circumstance? See CCC 227.

3. Look up the following verses. What does each teach you about walking through darkness?

   A. Deuteronomy 31:6

---

[4] Jolie Lee, "Biggest American Fear? Walking Alone at Night, Survey Finds," *USA Today*, October 22, 2014, http://www.usatoday.com/story/news/nation-now/2014/10/22/fear-study-chapman-university/17663861/.

B. Psalm 27:1 and John 8:12

C. Isaiah 41:10

D. Romans 8:28

4. Which of these verses helps you the most in dealing with your fears? Write it down on an index card and carry it with you.

Quiet your heart and enjoy His presence. . . . God does His finest work in the darkness.

"God has to work in the soul in secret and in darkness because if we fully knew what was happening and what Mystery, transformation, God and Grace will eventually ask of us, we would either try to take charge or stop the whole process." —Saint John of the Cross

The deepest soul work is done in the darkness, and it isn't a group exercise. There are times when God allows us to go to places that we wouldn't choose to go, because it is only there that we will be transformed in the most beautiful of ways. But we shouldn't be afraid of this, because God accompanies us there. We never walk in darkness alone. True, we may feel alone. But our feelings don't define reality. God does. And He promises never to leave us. He is there in the secret places in a way that our minds don't really comprehend.

Take the verse you chose for question 4 and personalize it. Turn it into a prayer of thanksgiving. For example, using Isaiah 41:10, you could pray:

Dear Lord,

Thank you for making it so that I do not need to be afraid, because you are with me. I don't need to be anxious, because you are my God. Thank you for strengthening me. Thank you for helping me. Thank you for upholding me with your victorious right hand. Thank you for grasping hold of me and never letting me go.

Day Three
AFRAID OF REJECTION

We don't always recognize this as a personal struggle because we don't connect the fear of rejection with its fruits. This fear manifests itself as people pleasing, approval seeking, a heightened sensitivity to criticism, feelings of worthlessness, and a rejection of others so that we turn away before they do. We need to get to the root of this fear if we want to walk in freedom.

1. How does Proverbs 29:25 describe "fear of man" or "fear of others"? Note: The phrase used in the Bible to describe being a people pleaser or caring too much what others think of us is "fear of man."

A snare is a trap that typically has a noose of wire or a cord. Caring too much what others think is a snare that strangles our freedom. It causes us to crave approval and fear rejection, and puts people in a place meant for God alone.

2. We all experience rejection at some point in our lives. It's unavoidable. But being afraid of it or totally train wrecked by it is actually optional. It all boils down to what our identity is based on. If the way our worth is defined is through people's acceptance of us, then fear of rejection will always be a noose around our necks. But if we can totally embrace the truth that **people's opinions do not determine our worth or identity, that our worth is determined by God and our identity is rooted in being His beloved daughter**, then freedom can be ours.

   God's approval is the only one that ultimately matters, and He *adores you*. Yes, *you*. You are not an exception to the rule, no matter what you've done or what you're struggling with today.

   What insight do the following verses give as we seek to please God and find our identity in Him?

   Romans 8:31

Galatians 1:10

Colossians 3:23

3. Do you struggle with a fear of rejection? If so, in what specific way? (Typical manifestations of this fear are people pleasing, approval seeking, sensitivity to criticism, feelings of worthlessness, tendency to reject others.)

Quiet your heart and enjoy His presence. . . . Do you want to see God show up in your life in a powerful way? Are you tired of the status quo and ready for more? Would you like to see God, in all His glory, intersect your circumstances?

God wants us to experience His glory. He wants to pour out His power on us and to see us living freed, transformed lives. This has always been His desire. When Jesus walked the earth, there was nothing He wanted more—for the people to see His glory and to be changed as a result. But so many of them missed it. Why? The reason is found in the Gospel of John: "for they loved the praise of men more than the praise of God." (John 12:43) They wanted something more than God's power and glory. They wanted human praise.

Jesus is turning to you now and asking, "What do you want?" How will you answer Him?

Day Four
AFRAID TO LEAN IN TO JOY

"What if I fall?
Oh, my darling, what if you fly?"[5]

1. Jesus came to set us free from the fears that hold us back from soaring as God's beloved daughters. How is the life He desires for us described in the following verses?

John 10:10

1 Timothy 6:17 (the second part of the verse)

Isaiah 30:18

These verses paint a picture of God wanting us to live deeply satisfying, meaningful, joy-filled lives. These are God's own words, so we can count on them as truth.

But how often do we believe the lies instead? All too often, we don't see God as a gracious, generous father. We believe the lie that He's going to hold out on us (this, of course, was the thought that got things spiraling out of control in the Garden of Eden). Some of us believe the lie that God is a disinterested father. Disaster might be just around the corner, but He's too busy with other things to do anything about it.

Believing lies about God really messes with our ability to embrace and live the life we were created for.

Have you ever realized that your life is going pretty well, and instead of resting in the joy of that moment and thanking God for all He's given, you think, "Oh, no! The other shoe is about to drop"? In her vulnerability research, Dr. Brené Brown has found that the most terrifying, difficult emotion we experience is *joy*. We're afraid to

---

[5] Erin Hanson, "Just My Poems," The Poetic Underground,
   http://thepoeticunderground.com/post/87639964775/the-talent-of-all-of-you-astounds-me-this-a-quote.

lean in to joy, because the thought of it being taken away is so scary. She describes our mental response as "dress-rehearsing tragedy":

> Dress rehearsing tragedy, she explains, is imagining something bad is going to happen when in reality, nothing is wrong. "How many of you have ever stood over your child while they're sleeping and thought, 'Oh . . . I love you'—and then pictured something horrific happening?" Brown asks. "Or woke up in the morning and thought, 'Oh my gosh, job's going great. Parents are good. This can't last.'"[6]

This isn't how God wants us to live. He wants us to lean in to joy and soar! So how do we do that? How can we break free of our tendency to pull back in fear and miss our lives because we are living in the gray?

2. We spent Lesson 12 learning about the Eucharist. Hidden in its meaning is one of the ways we can lean in to the joy we were created for. *Eucharist* means "thanksgiving." Practicing gratitude is one of the best ways to live a life of joy.

List an area of life where you fear something that is currently wonderful going awry. What are you afraid of specifically?

Practice gratitude by listing all the things you are grateful for about that very area of life.

It's up to you. You decide which of those lists you are going to dwell on. One will leave you paralyzed by the fear of "what if." The other will lead you to joy.

3. Underneath our reluctance to really embrace joy is the fear that we will fall. And consciously or not, we figure that the higher the place we're falling from, the more it will hurt. So we climb down from the peak of joy and sit in the middle ground of low expectations because it feels safer. And life passes us by.

---

[6] "Brené Brown: 'Joy Is the Most Vulnerable Emotion We Can Experience,'" *Huffington Post*, October 27, 2013, http://www.huffingtonpost.com/2013/10/18/brene-brown-joy-numbing-oprah_n_4116520.html.

I can't promise you that you will never fall or that life will never bring you pain. But God makes us promises in Scripture that should make an enormous difference in the way we live. In Deuteronomy 33:27, He promises, "The eternal God is your dwelling place, and underneath are the everlasting arms." Write that verse below. Think about it. Why does this truth matter? What difference does it make to you personally?

Quiet your heart and enjoy His presence. . . . The Lord is your refuge.

Have you whispered these questions?

"What if I fall?"
"What if I fall because of disappointment?"
"What if I fall because of tragedy?"
"What if I fall because I'm just not good enough?"

Lean in and listen, my friend. If you fall, God will catch you. It's as simple as that. He promises that underneath you, no matter what height you are falling from, He will catch you in His everlasting arms. What do we find at the end of our resources, the end of our dreams, the end of our hopes? We find God's mercy. We find God's graciousness. We find shelter from the storm.

That shelter is available to you right now. "He will cover you with his pinions, and under his wings you will find refuge." (Psalm 91:4) Come under His wings in prayer. Rest in safety.

"Because he clings to me in love, I will deliver him; I will protect him, because he knows my name. When he calls to me, I will answer him; I will be with him in trouble, I will rescue him and honor him. With long life I will satisfy him, and show him my salvation." (Psalm 91:14–16)

Rest in these promises.

Don't miss your life.

Appendix 1
SAINT THÉRÈSE OF LISIEUX
Patron Saint of Walking with Purpose

Saint Thérèse of Lisieux was gifted with the ability to take the riches of our Catholic faith and explain them in a way that a child could imitate. The wisdom she gleaned from Scripture ignited a love in her heart for her Lord that was personal and transforming. The simplicity of the faith that she laid out in her writings is so completely Catholic that Pope Pius XII said, "She rediscovered the Gospel itself, the very heart of the Gospel."

Walking with Purpose is intended to be a means by which women can honestly share their spiritual struggles and embark on a journey that is refreshing to the soul. It was never intended to facilitate the deepest of intellectual study of Scripture. Instead, the focus has been to help women know Christ: to know His heart, to know His tenderness, to know His mercy, and to know His love. Our logo is a little flower, and that has meaning. When a woman begins to open her heart to God, it's like the opening of a little flower. It can easily be bruised or crushed, and it must be treated with the greatest of care. Our desire is to speak to women's hearts no matter where they are in life, baggage and all, and gently introduce truths that can change their lives.

Saint Thérèse of Lisieux, the little flower, called her doctrine "the little way of spiritual childhood," and it is based on complete and unshakable confidence in God's love for us. She was not introducing new truths. She spent countless hours reading Scripture and she shared what she found, emphasizing the importance of truths that had already been divinely revealed. We can learn so much from her:

> The good God would not inspire unattainable desires; I can, then, in spite of my littleness, aspire to sanctity. For me to become greater is impossible; I must put up with myself just as I am with all my imperfections. But I wish to find the way to go to Heaven by a very straight, short, completely new little way. We are in a century of inventions: now one does not even have to take the trouble to climb the steps of a stairway; in the homes of the rich, an elevator replaces them nicely. I, too, would like to find an elevator to lift me up to Jesus, for I am too little to climb the rough stairway of perfection. So I have looked in the books of the saints for a sign of the elevator I long for, and I have read these

words proceeding from the mouth of eternal Wisdom: "He that is a little one, let him turn to me" (Proverbs 9:16). So I came, knowing that I had found what I was seeking, and wanting to know, O my God, what You would do with the little one who would answer Your call, and this is what I found:

"As one whom the mother caresses, so will I comfort you. You shall be carried at the breasts and upon the knees they shall caress you" (Isaiah 66:12–13). Never have more tender words come to make my soul rejoice. The elevator which must raise me to the heavens is Your arms, O Jesus! For that I do not need to grow; on the contrary, I must necessarily remain small, become smaller and smaller. O my God, You have surpassed what I expected, and I want to sing Your mercies. (Saint Thérèse of the Infant Jesus, *Histoire d'une Ame: Manuscrits Autobiographiques* [Paris: Éditions du Seuil, 1998], 244.)

Appendix 2
CONVERSION OF HEART

The Catholic faith is full of beautiful traditions, rituals, and sacraments. As powerful as they are, it is possible for them to become mere habits in our lives, instead of experiences that draw us close to the heart of Christ. In the words of Saint John Paul II, they can become acts of "hollow ritualism." We might receive our first Communion and the sacraments of confession and confirmation, yet never experience the interior conversion that opens the heart to a personal relationship with God.

Pope Benedict XVI has explained that the "door of faith" is opened at one's baptism, but we are called to open it again, walk through it, and rediscover and renew our relationship with Christ and His Church.[7]

So how do we do this? How do we walk through that door of faith so we can begin to experience the abundant life that God has planned for us?

GETTING PERSONAL

The word *conversion* means "the act of turning." This means that conversion involves a turning away from one thing and a turning toward another. When you haven't experienced conversion of heart, you are turned *toward* your own desires. You are the one in charge, and you do what you feel is right and best at any given moment. You may choose to do things that are very good for other people, but the distinction is that *you are choosing*. You are deciding. You are the one in control.

Imagine driving a car. You are sitting in the driver's seat, and your hands are on the steering wheel. You've welcomed Jesus into the passenger's seat, and have listened to His comments. But whether or not you follow His directions is really up to you. You may follow them or you may not, depending on what seems right to you.

When you experience interior conversion, you decide to turn, to get out of the driver's seat, move into the passenger's seat, and invite God to be the driver. Instead of seeing Him as an advice giver or someone nice to have around for the holidays, you give Him control of every aspect of your life.

---

[7] Pope Benedict XVI, *Apostolic Letter: Porta Fidei*, for the Indiction of the Year of Faith, October 11, 2011.

More than likely, you don't find this easy to do. This is because of the universal struggle with pride. We want to be the ones in charge. We don't like to be in desperate need. We like to be the captains of our ships, charting our own courses. As William Ernest Henley wrote, "I am the master of my fate: I am the captain of my soul."

Conversion of heart isn't possible without humility. The first step is to recognize your desperate need of a savior. Romans 6:23 states that the "wages of sin is death." When you hear this, you might be tempted to justify your behavior, or compare yourself with others. You might think to yourself, "I'm not a murderer. I'm not as bad as this or that person. If someone were to put my good deeds and bad deeds on a scale, my good ones would outweigh the bad. So surely I am good enough? Surely I don't deserve death!" When this is your line of thought, you are missing a very important truth: Just one sin is enough to separate you from a holy God. Just one sin is enough for you to deserve death. Even your best efforts to do good fall short of what God has required in order for you to spend eternity with Him. Isaiah 64:6 says, "All our righteous deeds are like a polluted garment." If you come to God thinking that you are going to be accepted by Him based on your "good conduct," He will point out that your righteousness is nothing compared to His infinite holiness.

Saint Thérèse of Lisieux understood this well, and wrote, "In the evening of my life I shall appear before You with empty hands, for I do not ask You to count my works. All our justices are stained in Your eyes. I want therefore to clothe myself in Your own justice and receive from Your love the eternal possession of Yourself."[8]

She recognized that her works, her best efforts, wouldn't be enough to earn salvation. Salvation cannot be earned. It's a free gift. Saint Thérèse accepted this gift, and said that if her justices or righteous deeds were stained, then she wanted to clothe herself in Christ's own justice. We see this described in 2 Corinthians 5:21: "For our sake he made him to be sin who knew no sin, so that in him we might become the righteousness of God."

How did God make Him who had no sin to be sin for you? This was foretold by the prophet Isaiah: "But he was wounded for our transgressions, he was bruised for our iniquities; upon him was the chastisement that made us whole, and with his strips we are healed." (Isaiah 53:5)

---

[8] Saint Thérèse of Lisieux, "Act of Oblation to Merciful Love," June 9, 1895.

Jesus accomplished this on the cross. Every sin committed, past, present, and future, was placed on Him. Now, *all the merits of Jesus can be yours*. He wants to fill your empty hands with His own virtues.

But first, you need to recognize, just as Saint Thérèse did, that you are little. You are weak. You fail. You need forgiveness. You need a savior.

When you come before God in prayer and acknowledge these truths, He looks at your heart. He sees your desire to trust Him, to please Him, to obey Him. He says to you, "My precious child, you don't have to pay for your sins. My Son, Jesus, has already done that for you. He suffered, so that you wouldn't have to. I want to experience a relationship of intimacy with you. I forgive you.[9] Jesus came to set you free.[10] When you open your heart to me, you become a new creation![11] The old you has gone. The new you is here. If you will stay close to me, and journey by my side, you will begin to experience a transformation that brings joy and freedom.[12] I've been waiting to pour my gifts into your soul. Beloved daughter of mine, remain confident in me. I am your loving Father. Crawl into my lap. Trust me. Love me. I will take care of everything."

This is conversion of heart. This act of faith lifts the veil from your eyes and launches you into the richest and most satisfying life. You don't have to be sitting in church to do this. Don't let a minute pass before opening your heart to God and inviting Him to come dwell within you. Let Him sit in the driver's seat. Give Him the keys to your heart. Your life will never be the same again.

---

[9] "If we confess our sins, he is faithful and just, and will forgive our sins and cleanse us from all unrighteousness." 1 John 1:9

[10] "So if the Son makes you free, you will be free indeed." John 8:36

[11] "Therefore, if any one is in Christ, he is a new creature; the old has passed away, behold, the new has come." 2 Corinthians 5:18

[12] "I will sprinkle clean water upon you, and you shall be clean from all your uncleannesses, and from all your idols I will cleanse you. A new heart I will give you, and a new spirit I will put within you; and I will take out of your flesh the heart of stone and give you a heart of flesh." Ezekiel 36:25, 26

Quit Hustling.
Find Peace.

 Are you ready to trade proving and pleasing for belonging and breathing deeply?

 Are you longing to exhale?

 Are you tired of pressure and longing for joy?

Scan here for a free audio talk
on 4 ways to quit
hustling and find peace!

*This free, exclusive content will put you
on the road to your happiest year yet!*

Appendix 3
ANSWER KEY

Lesson 1, Day One
1. Conversion is the first work of the grace of the Holy Spirit. It is grace that moves man to turn toward God and away from sin.
2. Justification is not only the remission of sins but also the sanctification and renewal of the interior man. Justification *detaches man from sin*. It purifies his heart of sin. It reconciles man with God. It frees him from the enslavement to sin. Justification heals.
3. We are saved through the bath of rebirth and renewal by the Holy Spirit. The bath of rebirth is baptism. He poured out the Holy Spirit on us so we could be justified by His grace and become heirs in hopes of eternal life.
4. As we saw in question 3, according to Titus 3:4–7, we need to experience rebirth and renewal by the Holy Spirit (baptism) to experience all the benefits of justification. We read in CCC 1991 that we also need to accept "God's righteousness through faith in Jesus Christ." This is what we do when we "make our faith our own." We receive God's grace in baptism. But many of us walked away from Him at some point, and are trying to find our way back to Him. This is why we need to experience conversion of heart, a true turning back to God. We ask Him to pour His faith, hope, and love into our hearts. We ask for Him to fill us. We recognize that it's God's righteousness that we need, because our own just isn't enough.

Lesson 1, Day Two
1. We cannot earn the grace of salvation. It is a gift from God.
2. Our salvation (justification) comes at an enormous cost: Christ's life. "Justification has been merited for us by the Passion of Christ . . ." (CCC 1992)
3. The charity (or love) of Christ *in us* is the source of all our merits before God. Grace is what unites us to Christ in love. It ensures that our acts have supernatural impact and value.
4. Perhaps we simply have difficulty with the concept of something being given that is truly undeserved. Even as we accept Christ's forgiveness and gift of salvation, we remain aware of the things we have done that were good. Our tendency to self-justify and feel a little superior to others is strong. At the same time, we're quick to attribute ill motive to others and to notice when we think they don't deserve mercy or help. This is what Jesus was talking about when He asked, "How can you say to your brother, 'Brother, let me take out the speck that is in your eye,' when you yourself do not see the log that is in your own eye?" (Luke 6:42)

Lesson 1, Day Three
1. Sin is not to have power over us because we are not under the law but under grace.
2. The law was given so that every mouth would be silenced and the whole world stands accountable to God. We become conscious of our own sin through the law.
3. The new law is the grace of the Holy Spirit.
4. Answers will vary for the first two questions. Lack of prayer is always an indication that we are relying on ourselves instead of on God.

Lesson 1, Day Four
1. God told Saint Paul that His grace was sufficient for him, because God's power was made perfect in weakness.
2. We receive grace through the sacraments.

3. Saint Paul was content with the thorn in his life—not just this particular thorn but also weaknesses, insults, hardships, persecution, and constraints, because he had learned that when he was weak, he was actually strong; his dependence on the Lord unleashed God's power within him.

Lesson 2, Day One
1. Peter took his eyes off of Jesus and focused on the waves. He was saved from drowning because Jesus reached out His hand and caught him.
2. He's given us a spirit of power, love, and self-control.
3. Answers will vary.

Lesson 2, Day Two
1. No. Jesus said that in this world we'll actually have trouble. But He encouraged us to take heart, because He has overcome the world.
2. She learned that everything passes; our troubles have an end date. Only God never changes. If we are patient in our difficulties, we'll learn that God alone is enough.
3. **A.** We don't walk alone. This passage encourages us to be strong and steadfast; to have no fear, for it is the Lord, our God, who marches with us; He will never fail us or forsake us.
   B. In Jesus' presence, we are never in darkness. He is our light and He promises to save us. Because He is with us, we don't need to be afraid.
   C. God is always with us. He promises to always strengthen and uphold us.
   D. Nothing can separate us from the love of God. Nothing.
4. Answers will vary.

Lesson 2, Day Three
1. It's described as a snare.
2. **Romans 8:31** Ultimately, it's only God's opinion that matters. And the Creator of the universe is *for us*.
   Galatians 1:10 We have a choice. We can either seek to please people or seek to please God. We can't have it both ways.
   Colossians 3:23 Whatever we do, our motive for doing it should be to please God, not to try to meet the expectations of people around us.
3. Answers will vary.

Lesson 2, Day Four
1. **John 10:10** It's described as an abundant life.
   1 Timothy 6:17 It's described as a life in which all the things God has provided for us are for our enjoyment.
   Isaiah 30:18 It's described as a life in which the Lord is waiting to be gracious to us, to show us mercy.
2. Answers will vary.
3. Answers will vary.

"For to the one who has, more will be given"
Matthew 13:12

The Journey Doesn't End Here

~ Christ's Love Is Endless ~

Walking with Purpose is more than a Bible study, it's a supportive community of women seeking lasting transformation of the heart. And you are invited.

Walking with Purpose believes that change happens in the hearts of women – and, by extension, in their families and beyond – through Bible study and community. We welcome all women, irrespective of faith background, age, or marital status.

Connect with us online for regular inspiration and to join the conversation. There you'll find insightful blog posts, videos, and free scripture printables.

For a daily dose of spiritual nourishment, join our community on Facebook, Twitter, Pinterest and Instagram.

And if you're so moved to start a Walking with Purpose study group at home or in your parish, take a look at our website for more information.

walkingwithpurpose.com

walking with purpose
⌒ SO MUCH MORE THAN A BIBLE STUDY ⌒

❊ DEEPEN YOUR FAITH ❊ OPEN YOUR ARMS ❊ ❊ BROADEN YOUR CIRCLE ❊

When your heart opens, and your love for Christ deepens, you may be moved to bring Walking With Purpose to your friends or parish. It's rewarding experience for many women who, in doing so, learn to rely on God's grace while serving Him.

If leading a group seems like a leap of faith, consider that you already have all the skills you need to share the Lord's Word:

- Personal commitment to Christ
- Desire to share the love of Christ
- Belief in the power of authentic, transparent community

The Walking With Purpose community supports you with:

- Training
- Mentoring
- Bible study materials
- Promotional materials

Few things stretch and grow our faith like stepping out of our comfort zone and asking God to work through us. Say YES, soon you'll see the mysterious and unpredictable ways He works through imperfect women devoted to Him.

Remember that if you humbly offer Him what you can, He promises to do the rest.

"See to it that no one misses the grace of God" Hebrews 12:15

Learn more about bringing Walking with Purpose to your parish. Visit us at walkingwithpurpose.com

Walking with Purpose
Seven Priorities that Make Life Work

Does your life feel out of control? Do you feel that you are doing so many things that you are doing none of them well? Did you know that Lisa Brenninkmeyer wrote a book to help you uncover the key to living a busy life with inner calm?

With humor and wisdom, Lisa will help you:

- **Stop striving and rest in God's unconditional love**
- **Experience new hope in your marriage**
- **Reach your child's heart**
- **Create clarity in a cluttered home**
- **Find friendships that go below the surface and satisfy**
- **Discover your passion and purpose**

Study Guide also Available

The book, *Walking with Purpose: Seven Priorities that Make Life Work,* and the accompanying Discussion Guide make up a 6-week study you can do on your own or with a group of friends.

Get your copy of Lisa's book,
***Walking with Purpose:*
*Seven Priorities that Make Life Work,***
at shop.walkingwithpurpose.com

walking with purpose

Walking with Purpose Devotionals

Daily affirmations of God's love

Rest: 31 Days of Peace

- A beautiful, hardcover, pocket-sized devotional to take wherever you go.
- 31 Scripture-based meditations that you can read (and re-read) daily.
- Become saturated with the truth that you are seen, known, and loved by a God who gave everything for you!

Be Still: A Daily Devotional to Quiet Your Heart

- Grow closer to the Lord each day of the year with our 365-day devotional.
- This beautifully designed hardcover devotional collection will renew your mind and help you look at things from God's perspective.
- Apply what you read in *Be Still*, and you'll make significant progress in your spiritual life!

shop.walkingwithpurpose.com

walking with purpose
SO MUCH MORE THAN A BIBLE STUDY

blaze for Tween/Teen Girls!

*Do you want to help girls grow
in confidence, faith and kindness?*

The Lord is calling for women like you to speak truth into the hearts of young girls – girls who can be easily confused about their true worth and beauty.

BLAZE is the Walking with Purpose ministry designed especially for tween/teen girls. It makes the wisdom of the Bible relevant to the challenges girls face today, and teaches them to recognize the difference between the loving voice of their heavenly Father and the voices that tell them they aren't good enough.

You can be a positive influence on the girls you know by starting a BLAZE program for any number of girls in your parish, school or home (or use one-on-one)!

The 20-week **BLAZE Core Program** includes a Leader's Guide and fun BLAZE kits. Each kit contains a pack of Truth vs. Lie cards, materials for icebreaker activities, take-home gifts and the BLAZE Prayer Journal.

You might also like **Between You and Me**, a 40-day conversation guide for mothers and daughters to read together. The daily reflection, journaling opportunities, discussion questions, and prayer prompts will help take your relationship to a new level of honesty and intimacy.

Discovering My Purpose is a six-lesson Bible study designed to open girls' eyes to their unique purpose, gifts, and God's love. It includes the **BLAZE Spiritual Gifts Inventory**, a fabulous tool to help girls discern where God is calling them to be world-changers.

Learn more at walkingwithpurpose.com/BLAZE

"BE WHO GOD MEANT YOU TO BE
AND YOU WILL SET THE WORLD ON FIRE."
SAINT CATHERINE OF SIENA

walking with purpose

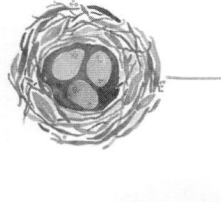

Transformative Catholic Bible Studies

Walking with Purpose Bible studies are created to help women deepen their personal relationship with Christ. Each study includes many lessons that explore core themes and challenges of modern life through the ancient wisdom of the Bible and the Catholic Church.

Opening Your Heart

A thoughtful consideration of the fundamental questions of faith – from why and how to pray to the role of the Holy Spirit in our lives and the purpose of suffering.

Living In the Father's Love

Gain a deeper understanding of how God's unconditional love transforms your relationship with others, with yourself, and most dearly, with Him.

Keeping In Balance

Discover how the wisdom of the Old and New Testaments can help you live a blessed lifestyle of calm, health, and holiness.

Touching the Divine

These thoughtful lessons draw you closer to Jesus and deepen your faith, trust, and understanding of what it means to be God's beloved daughter.

Discovering Our Dignity

Modern-day insight directly from women of the Bible presented as a tender, honest, and loving conversation—woman to woman.

Beholding His Glory

Old Testament Scripture leads us directly to our Redeemer, Jesus Christ. Page after page, God's awe-inspiring majesty is a treasure to behold.

Beholding Your King

This study of King David and several Old Testament prophets offers a fresh perspective of how all Scripture points to the glorious coming of Christ.

Grounded In Hope

Anchor yourself in the truth found in the New Testament book of Hebrews, and gain practical insight to help you run your race with perseverance.

Fearless and Free

With an emphasis on healing and wholeness, this study provides a firm foundation to stand on, no matter what life throws our way.

Reclaiming Friendship

Let God reshape how you see and experience intentional relationships, deal with your past friendship wounds, and become a woman who is capable of the lifelong bond of true friendship.

Ordering Your Priorities

An immensely practical study that will help you put the most important things first. Discover not only what matters most in life, but also how to prioritize those things!

**Choose your next Bible study at
shop.walkingwithpurpose.com**

walking with purpose
SO MUCH MORE THAN A BIBLE STUDY

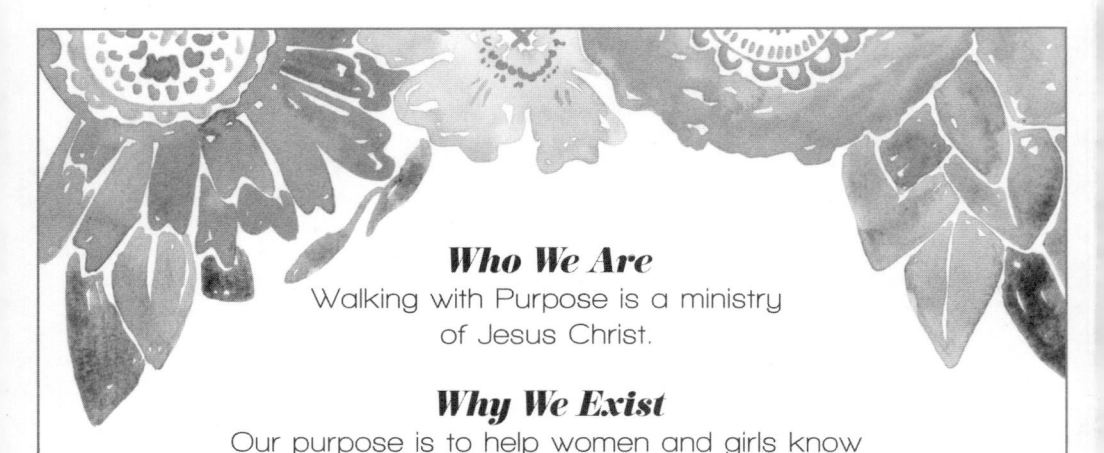

Who We Are

Walking with Purpose is a ministry
of Jesus Christ.

Why We Exist

Our purpose is to help women and girls know
Jesus Christ personally by making Scripture and the
teachings of the Catholic Church relevant and applicable.

Our Mission

Our mission is to help every Catholic woman and girl in
America encounter Jesus Christ through our Bible studies.

Our Vision

Our vision for the future is that, as more Catholic
women deepen their relationships with Jesus Christ,
eternity-changing transformation will take place in their
hearts — and, by extension — in their families, in their
communities, and ultimately, in our nation.

walking with purpose
SO MUCH MORE THAN A BIBLE STUDY

You can support our mission through a tax-deductible gift.
Learn more at walkingwithpurpose.com/donate